EXPLORE NORTH NORFOLK COAST

EXPLORE THE NORTH NORFOLK COAST

By
Ian Lyall

2nd edition

©Ian Lyall, April 2014

Published by Lulu Enterprises
26-28, Hammersmith Grove
London W6 7BA

ISBN: 978-1-291-82069-0

FOREWARD TO 2nd EDITION

I still have the same love for this coast that I confessed to when I published the first edition in 2007.

The countryside still has that beauty, peace and tranquillity that it possessed then, though it has become evermore popular.

But I have decided on a revision as in the first place there have been inevitable changes over a period of seven years and I wish to rectify these.

Also I take recognition that I can not hope to compete in a market of large format/full-page colour illustrations.

This volume has thus a smaller page size than its predecessor. Additionally I have chosen to use, for illustration, black-and-white photographs.

The coast was badly battered by the tidal floods of December 2013, but it is fighting back and restoration works are well afoot. The question does remain about the viability of coastal defences.

Ian Lyall, 5th April, 2014

v

INTRODUCTION

This book introduces you to the North Coast of Norfolk, to its many attractive towns and villages, its many interesting feature. It also helps guide you around this area.

We see on this coast a sample of the beauty of God's Creation, for that, rather what the geologists and other earth scientists would tell us, nor those who would tell us we revel in the beauty of 'Mother Nature'

Truly this land of wide-open spaces, with its sky- and seascapes forms the backdrop to what is a haven of peace and tranquillity. Surely this is what we need in an age of increasing stress and complexity, when the pace of life is for ever getting more hectic. Well has this coast been designated an 'Area of Outstanding Natural Beauty'. Here we have no stunning mountain views for example. Rather it is a place of open spaces, big skies and marvellous sunsets.

North Norfolk is a unique area in Britain. Its coast has its unique appeal. It has no major popular holiday resort and is a haven of peace and tranquillity. It is a great area for walking, using the North Norfolk Coast Footpath. It used to be possible to walk for hours and hardly meet another living soul- not quite the case today, but the area has not lost its appeal. It is a coast of big skies, great skyscapes and magnificent sunsets.

In summer with a south wind some of the highest temperatures in Britain may be recorded, but the North Wind can blow straight down from the North Pole. Even in mid-summer it can be decidedly cold. But given a quiet day and clear skies, even winter days can feel mild. One of the appeals of the area is the flint used in so many buildings, which give the many coastal villages their unique appeal. Many of these villages used to be thriving ports, but as the rivers have silted up, the sea has receded, and today only Wells-next-the-Sea remains a working harbour.

Visit the North Norfolk coast and you enter time warp. Life is lived at a slower pace. Go into a local shop for 'quick' service and you will find yourself caught up in a lengthy conversation.

The towns and villages of the

North Norfolk Coast

From Hunstanton to Brancaster

This section of the coast is tucked in the north-west corner of Norfolk, ranging from the popular resort of Hunstanton to quiet little villages, and apart from the cliffs in Hunstanton, the coast consists of sandy beaches beyond salt marshes.

HUNSTANTON

If anyone asks you in which town on the east coast of England, does the sun set over the sea, then the answer to this seeming riddle is Hunstanton.

Hunstanton faces out on to the 'Wash'. You find it just south of that point where the coast bends round to face more or less due north Today it is a modern seaside resort with all the bustle and activity associated with this. The long promenade (one of the finest; a broad walkway set some few feet above the sea) stretches south a long way beyond the limits of Hunstanton). Along here you can buy ice-cream, candyfloss, rock, there are amusements and all the trappings of the modern resort, and on the landward side of the Promenade lies a large area of caravan parks

Some little way long the Promenade you will come to the 'Kingdom of the Sea'. Here the visitor walks along tunnel-like passageways , surrounded not only on either side, but also above by giant aquaria in which swim all manner of rare and exotic forms of sea life.

From Hunstanton trips are available by boat out into the Wash, to Seal Island, where you can witness the seal colonies that inhabit these waters.

There are also a bowling green, indoor swimming pool and a theatre, and a well-known golf course.

Toward the northern end of the Promenade the 'Green' slopes down from the town centre. This is an area of grass, with seating available to sit and enjoy the surroundings and the sight over the expanse of sea stretching west, and on most days the opposing coast of Lincolnshire is visible. To the north and rising above the Green is an older Hunstanton; the resort of gentry of an earlier generation. This part lies atop the cliffs for which Hunstanton is justly famed, and which you may see if you go down onto the foreshore and walk north. Here you can see the three-tier cliffs, with strata coloured red, brown and white.

On top of these cliffs is a lighthouse dating back to 1841, but whose light last beamed out in 1921. Below the cliffs is a fine sandy beach.

Historical records tell us that in the winter of 1938 the sea froze off Hunstanton to a depth of 6 feet

The Promenade, Hunstanton; below The Green

OLD HUNSTANTON

Old Hunstanton offers a quieter, more secluded option for a holiday on this particular stretch of coast. It has an interesting relationship with the main town a mile to the south.

Old Hunstanton is a fishing village going back to the 9th century. From the Conquest, the Lords of the Manor were the Le Strange family. In 1860, Styleman Le Strange, realised an opportunity which presented itself with the coming of the railway, and a mile to the south built a resort, which was named 'New Hunstanton'. Now the roles are reversed. The old village is 'Old Hunstanton' whilst the 'New' resort is simple Hunstanton- which gained its seal of approval when the then Prince of Wales (later Edward VI) came here to convalesce.

The village has its own centre of interest, in the 'Old Strange Barns', where the attractions include craft demonstrations, including a working pottery.

To the east of the village, the cliffs give way to a sweeping sandy beach, whose dunes are a habitat for that Norfolk speciality: 'samphire'.

HOLME-NEXT-THE-SEA

Holme-next-the-Sea is a quiet village lying between the A149 coast road and its sandy beach, which is abutted at its western end by the Golf course of Hunstanton. Like so many of the sandy beaches of North Norfolk, this one is backed by dunes covered in marram grass.

Holme has a long history. Its earliest remain was discovered relatively recently, in the shape of what has been called 'Seahenge'. This consisted of an ancient tree ring of old timbers, with 55 oak posts. It was transferred to Fengate museum in Peterborough, where the laboratories carried out preservation work. Seahenge is believed to have been a religious relic dating from the Bronze Age.

Its importance in ancient times is underlined by the fact that it is the coastal terminus of an Iceni footpath, with its other end at Thetford in the south of Norfolk (in what is called 'Breckland'). The so-called Peddar's Way is now a waymarked path, and has been extended into a footpath along the coast- the 'North Norfolk Coastal Path'. This extends along the coast as far as Cromer.

Holme church is a typical flint building with the tall tower topped with brick battlements and pinnacles. On the south wall you will find an alabaster monument to one Richard Stone, who died in 1607 after 64 years of marriage, the progeny of which included seven sons and six daughters and went on to 72 grandchildren

Holme also has a nature reserve- Holme Bird Observatory, which is managed by the Norfolk Naturalist Trust, where there is a range of habitat and winter feeding stations. The Observatory is reached from the Coastal Path, or for Trust members along a road from the village.

THORNHAM

Thornham lies a mile inland from secluded sandy beaches, easily reached along the Coastal Path, and this is the shorter way to access the Bird Observatory at Holme. It lies at the end of a tidal creek, and was up to the 19th century a thriving harbour.

The trade at this was of a somewhat nefarious kind, by way of smuggling. The fact that the villages along this stretch of coast are tucked out-of-the-way made them ideal for this, combined with their proximity to the coast of Holland on the other side of the North Sea. It appears that the smugglers would sink their contraband at the coast, and then at low water the goods would be carried inland, to be sold at the 'Lifeboat Inn'.

This inn, set just of the road leading down toward the coast is still active as a modern hotel, which has a restaurant which does a roaring trade.

TITCHWELL

Titchwell, like its neighbour, is about a mile inland from the coast, with, here, a sandy beach. It lies along the main A149 road, and seems to consist of pubs and hotels-outstanding among which is the Titchwell Manor Hotel, which lies on the south side of the road, raised up about 10 feet above, and with magnificent views across the marshes

This stretch of coast was at one time protected by a sea-wall, but this was washed away by the devastating floods on 31 January 1953. In the marshes left behind, a pair of Montagu Harriers was spotted breeding in 1970, which was the stimulus for the RSPB to open Titchwell

Reserve, now a major bird-watchers site, with its reserves stretching all the way to the coast. It is provided with an ample car-park and a well resourced Visitor Centre.

The church of St Mary the Virgin has a flint-built round tower dating from the 11th Century.

BRANCASTER

Brancaster and its sister village extend for well over a mile along the main coast road. Its flint-built church stands at the cross-roads just as you enter the village from the west, and today is noted for the concerts staged in the church, with a full-scale musical festival at the middle weekend of June. International artists come to play here, especially on the twin manual organ made in 1912 by Wadsworth & Company of Leeds.

The beach at Brancaster is once again about a mile away from the village, reached here along a well-made road- a road which is subject to tidal flooding. There is ample parking space at the end, and a footpath leads alongside the clubhouse of the Golf Club. The beach is a broad strip of sand, backed by high dunes. Because it is so flat the beach can be dangerous as the tide comes in; the sea can move inland faster than a person can run.

Brancaster is home to the Royal West Norfolk Golf Club. This was founded in 1892. Its links can be cut off by the tide, and the course become an island, a fact for the erstwhile golfer to take into account.
Brancaster is the site of an ancient Roman fort, remains of which are still to be found in a field which lies between the main A149 and the Coastal Path. (The Roman name for Brancaster was *Branodunum*.)

BRANCASTER STAITHE

Brancaster runs along the coast road for about ½ mile, then after a short break (Note the AA call-box in the lay-by between the two- it is a listed building), you enter Brancater Staithe. The small harbour lies just 100yards left off the main road, and is a quay for a host of sailing vessels, and here you also find a National Trust office (The National Trust own and care for a considerable amount of Norfolk's North Coast.) Houses line either stretch of the main road and those on the seaward side have long gardens running down toward the salt marshes. They actually back on to the North Norfolk Coastal

Path. Between Brancaster and Brancaster Staithe the land is very marshy, but the path here is on a row of old railway sleepers, which makes for a much more comfortable walk, provided the hedge on the land-ward side is kept cut back. (I once had to turn back inn high summer, because it was virtually impossible to force a way through).

Mussels are collected along this stretch of coast, along with other shellfish, and on the walk down to the harbour you pass whelk-sheds, and you may well find yourself crunching the shells underfoot.

The village boasts a shop, two restaurants and a garage, where you can also buy daily papers and other more necessary items.

The harbour lies in a sheltered inlet, and off

Tree stumps, Thornham marshes

Burnham Deepdale Church

shore lies the nature reserve on Scolt Head Island. (see below)

SCOLT HEAD ISLAND

Scolt Head Island is a National Nature Reserve. An example of an offshore barrier island, it is difficult to access, and is best reached from Burnham Overy Staithe- ferries run between the months of April and October.

The main habitats on the island are sand dune, salt-marsh, intertidal sand and mudflats. It is home to a wide variety of ornithological life, with breeding Tern, and wintering wildfowl, among which are shellduck, widgeon, teal and curlew.

The chief plant-life is sea-lavender.

From Burnham Deepdale to Wells-next-the-Sea

BURNHAM DEEPDALE

There are seven 'Burnhams' altogether, and Deepdale is one of the smaller. (Burnham Market is the best known, whilst Horatio Nelson was born in Burnham Thorpe).

In fact it is virtually a continuation of Brancaster Staithe, and in common, lies on the main A149, with salt marshes and mudflats stretching down to the sea.

It possesses one of the oldest of the churches along this coast. Standing on the north side of the main road, you could almost miss it as you drive by. But this modest little church boasts a pre-Conquest round tower, a Norman font along with a collection of medieval glass. In the tower is hung a 15th century bell, cast by Thomas Derby of King's Lynn.

Horatio Nelson

"England expects every man to do his duty"

This is the supreme quotation associated with the man of the Royal Navy, who is widely regarded as being Norfolk's greatest son. These words were posted in flags on the mast of HMS Victory on the eve of the Battle of Trafalgar.

Nelson was born, the sixth of eleven children in Burnham Thorpe in 1758.

He became a sea captain at the age of 20 after eight years' service in the Royal Navy, having married Frances Nisbet at the age of 19. By then he has seen service in Canada, the Baltic and the West Indies. He returned to England with his wife on half-pay, frustrated at not being at sea. However the Napoleonic Wars were to see to that! In 1793 he was given charge of HMS Agamemnon. During service in the Mediterranean, he helped capture Corsica, then he, most famously, lost the sight of one eye during the Battle of Calvi, whilst in the Battle of Santa Cruz of Tenerife he lost his right arm.

In the Battle of Copenhagen in 1801, he disobeyed orders to cease fire, putting his telescope to his blind eye and declaring, "I see no ships"!

He successfully destroyed Napoleon's fleet in the Battle of the Nile (1798) Posted to Naples, he fell in love with Emily, Lady Hamilton, and though they never married they had a son, whom they named 'Horatio'. The same year Nelson was promoted as Vice-Admiral.

His most famous victory was the Battle of Trafalgar (1805) when he defeated Napoleon, but during the battle, he suffered fatal injuries.

BURNHAM OVERY STAITHE

This is most accurately just part of a larger parish- Burnham Overy, with the (larger) Burnham Overy Town ½ mile inland. This small village is about 1½ miles from the open sea which lies across salt marshes cut through by shallow channels. On the seaward side are quite high dunes, beyond which are fine sandy beaches- and these may be reach by way of the

Coastal Path.
In earlier times, when the channel was deeper, Overy Staithe was an active port.
Nowadays it is certainly very busy during the summer half of the year. The channel may be reached by a side road which runs one-way (east to west) off the main A149. During the winter half of the year, the main life is sea-bird life and the many waders which frequent this coast line
Half a mile to the west is a group of 18th century mill buildings grouped around the River Burn, as it meanders sea-ward, dominated by the black Burnham Overy windmill.

BURNHAM MARKET

Burnham Market is nowadays popularly known as 'Chelsea-by-the-Sea'- on account of its up-market sophistication. That a quiet Norfolk market town has thus developed is down in no small measure to the entrepreneurial skills of one man-the late Paul Whittome, owner of the Hoste Arms. This in itself was a village-green 'pub, but when Whittome bought it he had the vision to see what he could make of it- a hotel which in 2002 was listed as No 2 by *The Times*. Burnham Market is situated about 1½ miles from the coast, but regardless of the time of year, attracts hordes of visitors. This charming little town is becoming almost the victim of its

Overy Staithe

Burnham Market: The Green

own success. Its Green, lying at the centre, is jam-packed with parked cars, so much so that the parked vehicles spill over into the approach streets, and especially North Street.

The Green must be one of the most picturesque in the land, with cottages and larger houses of various periods. Running down the centre is the 'Goose Bec' which flows though Burnham and is channelled through before flowing into the River Burn. From time to time a spring tide coincides with a North wind, and the Bec floods the road through the Green.

There is a plethora of small businesses, most of them on the Green or in one of the side turns off it. Among the businesses, there are to be found baker, butcher, wine-merchant, a florist, a whole gamut of gift-shops (some of which are 'Aladdin's Caves' of everything under the sun), high fashion, antiques and an independent bookshop.

There is an abundance of accommodation, from holiday lets to a caravan site (this is near the old railway station), and restaurants- eg the 'Hoste', the 'Nelson'

St Mary's at the west end of the Green is the parish Church of Burnham Market. The decorations round the tower battlements show a potted version of the Bible. The original Parish Church is Burnham Westgate, a rather un-prepossessing church with a bell-cote standing on a junction about ¼ mile east of the Green.

Actually Burnham Market is an amalgamation of

three 'Burnhams'- Burnham Westgate, Burnham Ulph (named after a Danish chieftain who was brother of King Canute) and Burnham Market itself.

HOLKHAM

Holkham is in most people's minds Holkham Hall, which is the major and original part of Holkham Estate. However, originally Holkham was a village, and within the estate it still has its Post Office, and church.
The village lies on the main A149 road, with the Hall on the south side. Across the road is Holkham National Nature Reserve. This is the largest Reserve in England, stretching from the sandy beach, through pine trees on extended sand-dunes and all this backed by a mix of salt marshes and grazing land. The beach, which stretches all the way from Burnham Overy Staithe to Wells-next-the-Sea comprises golden sands, and this beach- like that at Brancaster is very flat and with tidal channels can be dangerous.
Holkham Beach is accessed by the Lady Anne Drive, which lies directly opposite the road into the Hall and grounds. This drive, which is over ½ mile long can park many cars, extending to that point where it crosses the North Norfolk Coast Path, here leading you just on the landward side of the pine-clad dunes. To the west is one of Britain's few naturist beaches.
On the Estate you will find a Bygones Museum,

a pottery shop (which houses the Post Office), teashop, a newly opened wine-cellar cum kitchen-ware shop and also the Victoria Hotel. The Estate has invested heavily in the area,

especially in Wells- owning a caravan park, bought from the North Norfolk District Council, and property in Wells. Along with Paul Whittome of Burnham Market's Hoste Arms, the Estate has done much to bring added value to the area, and bring this coast up-market.

HOLKHAM HALL

It was Thomas Coke, 1st Earl of Leicester, who built Holkham Hall. Begun in 1734 and built in the Palladian style, it reflects Coke's near-obsession with Italy, which he visited often, during his frequent 'Grand Tours' of Europe. It has been commented that Coke built the Hall to house the large collection of artistic artefacts which he brought home form his travels.
Coke employed Brettingham as architect to oversee the building, which was to be based on designs by William Kent, who was protégé of Lord Burlington, whom he had met in one of his visits to Rome.
The Hall we see today is substantially that which was completed in 1764. Only the vestibule which lies on the north side of the house, and the terraced gardens to the south were added later by the 2nd Earl during the

1850s.

The Hall is to this day still home to the Earls of Leicester. The house is closed to the public during the winter, but is open during the summer months (the Hall on certain days; the grounds, which are extensive are open most days.) It is a member of the Historic Houses Association.

HOLKHAM COUNTRY FAIR

Once every other year the Estate hosts the Holkham Country Fair.

It is held in the park on either side of the Hall. Held (normally) on the fourth weekend of July, it extends over Saturday and Sunday, and attracts 40,000 visitors.

From morning till evening each day there is a full programme of events for all ages, ranging from displays in the Grand Ring, through 200 trade stands, through aerobatic displays to helicopter rides over the area of the Estate. There are also plenty of 'have-a-go' activities, including clay-pigeon shooting and fishing to a children's playground

WELLS-NEXT-THE-SEA

Wells-next-the-Sea lies at the heart of the North Norfolk Coast, and is exactly halfway between Hunstanton and Sheringham.

It is no longer literally 'by-the-Sea'. The sea lies a full mile away (even more at Low Water), but the name recalls the time when Wells was near the sea and when it was an active and thriving port, and today some of the quayside warehouses still stand- converted now into luxury flats.

In fact Wells is still a working port-not the same degree as formerly, but a Harbour-Master's office is still on the quayside. A (decreasing) number of fishing boats still land their catch at the quay.

But Wells is first and foremost a holiday town.

Its resident population of about 2,500 is multiplied by a factor of three or four at the height of the holiday season. A stall on the Quay still sells cockles, mussels, shrimps and such like. Fish and chips are still to be had, but reflecting the changes on this whole coastline, the amusement arcades have gone. And Wells is still a centre for sailing, with extra moorings having been built in recent years.

Quite large vessels can make it through the (buoy-marked) narrow channel leading from the open sea, and often there is a tall-mast boat to be seen tied up. For the non-sailor, for those who just want to get to the beach there are various ways of getting there. Beach Road leads form the Quayside out to a car park on the land side of the dunes. For the pedestrian there is a footpath on the side of the embankment guarding the land-with magnificent views of the estuary, with its moored boats, sea birds and panoramas eastward as far as Blakeney. You can also get most of the way by the narrow-gauge railway which runs from the town end of Beach Road as far as the Pinewoods Caravan Park.- with just ¼ mile further on foot.

The town will hold your interest for long enough! It has so many and varied houses, nearly all flint-built, and to be found in a maze of narrow alleyways, many leading off the Quayside.

The shops of Wells are nearly all situated along Staithe Street. Apart from Leftley's supermarket (part of the 'Costcutter' chain) all are independent traders. There is a butcher, a fishmonger, a baker, a greengrocer, a chemist, and a whole row of shops will sell all manner of bric-a-brac, at give-away prices. There is the share of cafes, and Walsingham's which in two shops sell just about everything the holidaymaker might want. There are also shops on the Quay, including a delicatessen, and a

Wells, Coastal path through the pines

Tree felled by winter storm; Wells pines

Wells beach

The estuary, Wells

hand-made soap shop.

Not everything can be said about Wells without mentioning the Buttlands. This lies just beyond Staithe Street. It is a large rectangular Green lined with Georgian and Victorian houses, and two hotels.

At the bottom end of Staithe Street is a large Community Hall and theatre. Here are staged various craft fairs, book sales &c.

The grand St Nicholas' church is largely a 19th century rebuilding of an earlier gothic structure

The event of the year is Wells Carnival. Both residents and visitors are welcomed to take part in this week-long event, held often in the week spanning July and August. The highlight is Carnival Day when a procession of floats an with fancy dress makes its way through the town streets Traditional activities include a sandcastle competition and the crowning of the Carnival Queen.

Wells beach is sandy, though near the entry point the sand is muddy. Some 200-300 yards out to sea is a row of marram-grass covered dunes. Back against the pines is a long row of beach huts

Inland from Wells

There are many interesting little villages in the few miles south of Wells-next-the-Sea, leading to that village centre of Christian pilgrimage at Little Walsingham.

WARHAM

Warham is a quiet village lying just two miles south of Wells. Its charm lies in its many flint and cobble cottages, many adorned by beautiful well-kept gardens.

One attraction of Warham is the village pub, lying at a crossroads in the centre of the village, offering a first rate selection of home-made cooking to go with its ales and wines. You may well have to use the car-park in the field diagonally opposite, as the pub is too popular for the small parking area in front to cope.

Step inside and you are transported back to an earlier generation, with all sorts of artefacts from the early-mid 20th century.

Along the lane south of the village, about a mile along are the earthworks of an old iron-age fort, known as 'Warham Camp'.

WIGHTON

Wighton lies two miles further south of Warham. This little village has a pub, a post office and a tea shop. Sculptor Henry Moore has associations with the village; his sister taught in the local school and his father is buried in Wighton churchyard. He even practised his sculpture in the school yard.

LITTLE WALSINGHAM

Set in a picturesque landscape of rolling hills, this village is visited by Christians from all over the country.

It is a busy little village, but get away from the bustle and you will find it a charming little place. The High Street is full of gift and souvenir shops, and there is a tea room. At its northern end the street opens out into a square: 'Common Plain', where stands a 16th century pump, from which a pinnacle was broken off in 1900.

The church of St Mary was gutted by fire in 1961, but has been well restored. This church is not one of the points of pilgrimage, which centre round the three shrine churches. A mile to the south is the Roman Catholic 'Slipper Chapel', dating from the 14th century and the modern

Chapel of Reconciliation in Houghton St Giles. Within the village are the Anglican and Orthodox shrines.. The Anglican shrine church, set on a road junction is a modern building, surrounded by beautiful, peaceful gardens

The Anglican Shrine, Walsingham

From Stiffkey to Sheringham

This stretch of coast is, after the salt marshes of Stiffkey and Morston one characterised by shingle beaches. This makes the actual beach very difficult to walk along, and very uncomfortable to sit on. It is a quiet stretch of coast except in Blakeney, which is a hive of boating activities. Beyond Sheringham cliffs rise steeply above the shingle below.

STIFFKEY

The village of Stiffkey lies abreast the main A149 road, which makes a very difficult place for motorists. The village streets are very narrow, with flint walled cottages or just walls, and in quite few places there is scarcely room for two cars to pass: observe the 20mph speed-limit. But Stiffkey is a beautiful place set in the rolling country either side of the River Stiffkey, then on its seaward side all is different, with salt marshes stretching out to the sea; marshes which in wet weather or the autumn months can be very slippery.
At the east end of the village lies the gatehouse, the sole remains of Stiffkey Hall, home of the

Bacon family, and with their crest on the gatehouse. Nearby is the church of St John Baptist, best known on account of a former rector

MORSTON

Morston lies some ½ mile inland from the sea, behind an area of salt marshes, cut through by numerous inlets. If you follow the footpath from the quay out to sea you will find a narrow sandy strip. This is a desolate, isolated coast, with a beauty all its own. It has a rich variety of species of sea birds.

From the winding main street of the village there are several places where you can take one of the boat trips out to Blakeney Point to see the seals.

All Saints' church, is a Grade 2 listed building, and in the churchyard is a listed monument to the Butler family. The church is as famous for its commanding position on a bend of the main coast road as for its 15th century rood screen and 16th century font. Lightning struck the tower in 1743, which accounts for the odd appearance it presents for today.

BLAKENEY

In the 13th century, Blakeney was one of the top ten ports of England; its decline (in this respect) is down to the silting up of the estuary, which still reaches in to the quayside. Now more adjacent to the sea is Blakeney Point, where 1000 acres of sand dunes are home to a large number of seals. The Point, also a bird sanctuary, is cared for by the National Trust. Boats do go from Blakeney to the Point, though more frequent and convenient sailings are to be had from Morston.

The village is full of cobbled cottages, many of which are colour-washed, and the Main Street, sloping down toward the quayside has the air of a Cornish village. There is a range of shops, a pub, and a restaurant, and a large number of holiday-lets among the cottages.

The quayside car park (once run by the National Trust, but now by North Norfolk District Council) is a good starting point to walk out along an embankment overlooking the estuary, with its bird life and also very active yachting. The Guildhall opposite the quay is home to a craft exhibition and fair each summer.

Blakeney's major landmark is the parish church of St Nicholas. This is on account of its magnificent medieval tower, but also the narrow turret on the northeastern corner, which for many years acted as a lighthouse.

The chancel of this church was once that of a Carmelite friary. The original nave was replaced by today's grand nave about 1435. The six-bay nave rises to a magnificent hammer-beam roof. At the same time the 104-foot tower was built.

CLEY-NEXT-THE-SEA

Cley (pronounced 'Cly') is best known amongst the twitcher fraternity. Cley Marshes are home to a rich bird life; there are many migrant winter birds, and it is a place where many rare birds are seen, so much so that, to the east of the village is a look-out. When a rare bird is seen, the word goes out and soon bird-lovers from

The beach, Cley (above)

Morston creek (next page)

every corner of the land converge on Cley. The reed beds, which are home to the birds, lying between the shingle bank sea-defense, and the main A149 is managed by the Norfolk Naturalist Trust.

This is a busy little village, part of which lies on the A149 (here very narrow), but where the road makes a 90-degree left turn on entering from the west, another road extends the village well to the west, to the village's main pub.

Just left of the A149 at the east end of Cley is the famous mill. This 18th century example has had its timber sails replaced more than once, but it is a major landmark, and is now run as a guest-house, from the upper rooms of which are magnificent views across the marshes.

In the centre of the village is a magnificent delicatessen, and also an art gallery.

Out on the side-road you will eventually come to

Cley Church. St Margaret's church (dedicated to Margaret of Antioch) dates from the early 13th century. A church was begun on the site of an earlier one, and planned to be of some grandeur. The plans could not be completed on account of the Black Death. Even so, this is a magnificent church. The great West Window is one of the largest in Norfolk. Immediately in front of the window is a 15th century font (a Seven Sacrament font, on account that each of the seven sides displays one of the seven sacraments.) Beside the Lady Chapel is a pulpit made in 1611. In the chancel there are misericords, where tired monks would rest their weary bodies!). These are but a few of the many features to see in this still great church.

WIVETON

Wiveton is overlooked from Cley church. It lies in the Glaven valley, about a mile from both Blakeney and Cley. During the 16th and 17th centuries Wiveton lay by the sea. Great ships would have lain at anchor in its harbour. Then the tide would have flowed all the way to Glandford.
Inside St Mary's church, behind the Rector's reading desk, the stones were carved with ships from the 15th and 16th centuries. From the village green you may walk across Wiveton Down, an area of undulating scrubland.

SALTHOUSE

Salthouse is a conservation village, sitting alongside the main A149. It derives its name, quite logically from the fact that at one time there was a warehouse for locally-produced salt.

The salt marshes between the village and the shingle bank is home to may birds, and at the roadside is a pond where many birds (mostly ducks) may be observed, which get well fed by passing motorists, who stop alongside the pond and feed them.

The local pub is a centre for local birdwatchers. At one time there was a roadside cottage, from the window of which you could buy crab. This has now opened as a roadside restaurant where you can buy seafood salads at silly prices. There is no license, but visitors are welcome to take there own wine with them!

Behind and above the village is Salthouse Heath, which is an area of bracken and gorse, intersected by footpaths. The careful motorist can drive on to these and find somewhere to picnic and to admire the panoramic views over the sea.

KELLING

Kelling village spreads itself up a lane which begins off the A149, and on this corner there is a tea room, which also specialises in selling second-hand books.

Go through the village and continue on the road to take you on to Kelling Heath, which like its Salthouse counterpart is criss-crossed with a network of paths. On the Heath you will also find a collection of ancient burial mounds. Also on

the Heath is a station on the North Norfolk Railway, which runs from Holt to Sheringham.

Just along the coast is the 'Muckleborough Collection', which is on the site of an artillery range from World War II. The collection is of associated tanks and guns.

WEYBOURNE

Weybourne village is set in a mix of arable land and heathland, and makes an ideal area for walking.

Weybourne beach (shingle) is approached along a short pot-holed road leading off the A149 by the village stores, and near the church, known as 'Weybourne Priory'. When you reach

The cliff top, Weybourne

the car park you can either turn left and walk along the shingle, go down the shingle on to a sandy beach, or turn right and climb up on to Weybourne cliffs. These cliffs are facing serious erosion problems, and it is unwise to walk right up to the cliff edge. There is still a row of cottages, but each year these get a little nearer the cliff edge. Walk for about a mile and you arrive at one of the footpaths starting from Sheringham Park

Sheringham Park

HOLT

This wealthy Georgian market town lies about
2 ½ miles inland from the coast, but is integral
to the coastal region. It is definitely for the
discerning shopper. Butlers and Larners is an
independent department store, but the choice of
shops is legion. There is a fashion shop,
newsagent, chemist, independent bookshop,
several fish-and-ship outlets, and that names
but a few!
Most of the newer shops are in 'Appleyard', a
modern open-air shopping precinct. Here you
can get refreshments at a variety of outlets,

many of them with facilities for eating outdoors (weather permitting!)

Do not miss Picturecraft Art Gallery, which stages exhibitions several times a year, nearly all featuring local artists. There is a shop to buy painting materials adjacent.
If you need a supermarket, then there is Budgens, complete with shoppers' car park. This is the only chain outlet in Holt.
Take the road east out of the town and you will come to the railway station for the North Norfolk Railway. This was an enterprise by a group of local enthusiasts, who restored the track from Sheringham to Holt and run a regular service, including steam trains
There is a super delicatessen in the centre of the town, which has extended by first adding a cafe, then a modern restaurant and now bed-and-breakfast facilities. The time of the year to stay in Holt is when the Christmas lights are on; no gaudy show, but tasteful white lights everywhere.
Holt church of St Andrew's was gutted by fire early in the 18th century, rebuilt in 1727 and further developed by Butterfield.

SHERINGHAM

Three miles east of Weybourne is the town of Sheringham, which with some justice, describes itself as 'The prime coastal town of North Norfolk. From here on, the coast is quite different with a more commercial feel.

Sheringham itself was originally a fishing village, but was developed as a resort with the advent of the railway. Sheringham retains its 'Norfolk' character, and sits on top of the cliffs with steep walkways down to the beach, which, when the tide is out is sandy, but otherwise is strewn with an array of shells and pebbles.

In the town there is a range of art and craft outlets, and all the shops needed by what is a resident population of several thousand. As might be expected on this coast there are many fish shops, selling shell fish, also a range of restaurants

On the beach are all the usual accouterments of a popular seaside resort. The town also boasts its 'Little Theatre' and there is also the 'Sheringham Museum'

Seafront, Sheringham

NORTH NORFOLK COASTAL PATH

The North Norfolk Coastal Path was developed as an extension of the Peddars Way walk, which follows a track of prehistoric origins, that ran from Thetford north-west to the coast at Holme-next-the-Sea. It extends for a distance of 40 miles eastward along the coast to Cromer,

Here the path is described in its course from Thornham to Weybourne (some 28 miles of its length). Where streams and rivers have an outlet to the North Sea it is sometimes necessary for the track to move inland, sometimes as far as the A149 main road. Walkers should prepare themselves according to the weather and conditions underfoot are especially important. Whilst some sections follow well prepared surfaces, for much of its course it runs either along beaches, or (after Weybourne, for those going beyond to Sheringham or Cromer) on a grassy cliff top. Most of the way is across the salt marshes which characterise so much of this coast. Conditions underfoot can (especially in autumn to early spring, and dependant on recent weather) be very muddy. (Note: The footpath is clearly waymarked: follow the acorn way markers)

Thornham to Brancaster Staithe
From Thornham, the path takes you inland

across rolling agricultural land. When you reach the A149, cross carefully (the road can be very busy, especially in summer) and turn left for about 400 yards, and then turn right along a metalled road (Choseley Road) which climbs steadily upward to about 150 feet amsl. You will have excellent views behind you out to the sea. In 1 ¼ miles, you turn left by a small copse along a field track. You will cross two country lanes, before after another 700 yards turning left at a 'T' junction in the footpath. The way is now back downhill, until after passing the back of a cemetery you come into Brancaster. Cross the main road (again with care) - you will notice Brancaster church on the far right-hand corner. Just after the houses end, there is a gateway on the right, go through and you follow through onto a boarded walk which leads you after just over 1 mile into a grass field: cross this and come onto Brancaster Staithe.

Brancaster Staithe to Burnham Overy Staithe

Keeping past the Sailing Club, keep the general direction to pass along the backs of houses, with marshes on your left. The path turns left, then right in front of fencing, and so on to Deepdale Marsh. The road now follows sea-defences, curving gently right. Just under 2 miles, the path turns diagonally right. Continue along the defence bank and you will until you come to a 'T' junction, cross the river Burn and then in about 200 yards you come on to the A149. The footpath follows a field edge parallel to the road until you come after ½ mile to Burnham Overy Staithe, with a grassy bank overlooking Overy Creek

Burnham Overy Staithe to Wells-next-the-Sea

In Overy Staithe walk along the Harbour Way and at its eastern end as the road turns away to the right go through a gateway and after 100 yards, left on the sea-defence wall and head out northward. (On your right, the mudflats are rich with bird-life). The path turns right, then left until another paths joins from the right. The following 400 yards are very narrow and in winter very muddy and slippery. Eventually you come on to a boarded way which leads up into high dunes; across them you come on to a wide sandy beach. Walk out towards the water then bear right and follow the water line. After 1/2 mile you will see pinewoods to your right. The beach will curve right until 2 ¼ miles you reach Holkham Bay. Climb up onto the sand dunes and on to the boarded walkway which leads you for 200 yards through the pines on to the end of the Car Park on Lady Anne's Drive. Turn left through the gate, and follow the path along the southern side of the pines and dunes. After about 1 ½ miles, the footpath comes into an open area. Do not follow it southward; the Coastal Path branches off to the left and passes alongside the Pinewoods Caravan Park on to a Car Park, with adjacent shop and refreshment kiosk. Cross Beach Road at the end of the Car Park, climb on to the Sea Bank and head right. In 1 mile you come to Wells Harbour. Make you way alongside a Car Park on to the Quayside and turn left. The next 500mn yards are along Wells Quayside. At its end bear left on to East Quay

Wells-next-the-Sea to Morston

200yards along East Quay you come to a group of shacks. Pass the shacks on your left and then onto the Sea Defence and on to Warham Greens, which you enter turning left through a gateway on to a green swathe. At its end (after 2 miles) through the gate and 'Coclestrand Drove' will join from the right. In ½ mile you come to an N.T. sign 'Stiffkey Salt Marshes'. Pass an old military camp and then along the sandy track which continues to hug the edge of the marshes. After passing through marsh and gorse bushes, climb the bank over the River Stifffkey and continue across the marshes until after 2 ½ miles you reach Morston Harbour. (National Trust) Cross the open space of the harbour, past the N.T. office and on your right is the Coastal Path set on a grassy bank set above the marshes. Eventually dropping down to the level of the marshes (down some steps), bear left as another path joins from the right and follow along on to 'North Granary' which leads on to the quayside at Blakeney. Walk along the

Quayside until you come to the National Trust Car Park.

Blakeney to Cley-next-the-Sea

The distance by road is just over 1 mile: by the path it is much further. At the far end of the Car Park, back on to the sea-defence bank, but do not turn off over the stile on to the marsh. Follow the bank: eventually a fence will force you right and you will see Cley, with its famous windmill in front of you. The bank heads inland until it bears right at the A149. Stay on the bank if possible. Eventually you will have to join the footpath at the side of the busy A 149 into Cley

Cley-next-the-Sea to Weybourne

Follow the A149 through Cley. The road is twisting, narrow and busy- so do so WITH CAUTION. At the end of the village turn left into the Windmill Car Park. At its far RH end go up some steps, turn left down a bank, then right along the bottom of the bank. Turn right up on to the bank, along it to where it turns right, then down on to a lower bank. Follow this (left- toward the sea) until it reaches the main sea-defence bank (a high shingle bank).The footpath now follows the land side of the bank all the way to Kelling. You may, of course, climb the bank and on to the beach. (This is shingle and makes walking hard work for any distance!) Eventually after 3 ½ miles you will reach

Kelling, having passed Salthouse en route. At Kelling the shingle bank ends at a Car Park. Cross this and continue with the fence of a military installation on your right. Eventually you come to the shingle bank sheltering Weybourne, and come out on Weybourne Car Park. The route ends here: the Coastal Path continues, and if you wish to do so take the path which climbs up, and you will walk along the cliff top across grassy fields. DO NOT GO TOO CLOSE TO THE CLIFF EDGE

SOMEWHERE TO EAT AND SLEEP

The following is a list of places where my wife and I have eaten out along the North Norfolk coast. It is not, and cannot pretend to be an exhaustive list: in that sense exclusion is of no significance. We just hope the list will be helpful and you will find somewhere where you will enjoy a meal (Information was checked, so far as possible at the time of going to press: nor guarantees can be given)

The Lifeboat Inn, Thornham
Situated just off the road which leads from Thornham village to the coast is the Lifeboat Inn, which in bygone centuries was a hideout for smugglers. You can enjoy your food either in the cosy comfort of the "Smugglers' Hideout", or in the conservatory. Either way you get a choice from a wide-ranging menu which includes sea-food. Do be warned: the Lifeboat Inn is well-known and popular. It might pay to check on space availability or reserve a table.
tel: 01485 512 236

The Titchwell Manor Hotel

The Titchwell Manor is situated at the side of the main A149 coast-road. Although near the road it is raised about 10 feet above the marshes toward the sea; sufficient to afford magnificent views. It is a place to eat in style, and you can choose between the set menu and the blackboard. Expect an evening meal for two to cost £60-70 with a bottle of wine. Fish and sea-food play an important part on the menu.

You would be well advised to book; certainly for a weekend evening and in summer
tel: 01485 210 221

The Jolly Sailors, Brancaster Staithe

This pub has a good reputation for serving good-quality food. This can be eaten in the restaurant; there is also a beer garden at the rear and a family room, with more basic facilities food is served daily from 11am-11pm.. More info: (tel 01485-210314)

The White Horse Brancaster

More information: 01328-738777One of this coast's outstanding eating places. An excellent menu may be enjoyed in the spacious restaurant, out on a summer evening in the open area at the rear, raised up above and overlooking the sea marshes.

There is also accommodation. Its reputation is fully to be recommended.

Do expect to pay over £100 for a three-course meal with wine, for two
Contact: 01485-210262

The Hoste Arms, Burnham Market

Not the place to go to eat if you are watching your budget. The restaurant serves excellent food, the quality which is excellent with a good range of traditional and *a la cuisine* dishes.

If you wish to savour the lively flavour of the "Hoste", then maybe have a pre-meal drink in the public bar. If it's to your taste, then have a large glass of the house dry white wine.

There is a breath-taking range of accommodation, much in specially built annexes

The Globe Inn, Wells-next-the-Sea

The Globe has recently been upgraded by Holkham Estate. It offers an appetising selection of food, mainly light meals, but full courses are available. Enjoy inside in the modern décor, or outside in the courtyard, or at the front overlooking the 'Buttlands. The modernisation includes b&b facility

contact 01328710206

The Crown Hotel, Wells-next-the-Sea

Enjoy the fine fare prepared here: its won a place in the "Good Food Guide". The 16-th century hotel is situated in a far corner of the open grass area in Wells known as the Buttlands. The surroundings and décor are warm and welcoming, and there is now a conservatory at the rear

You will of course pay for quality and a three course meal for two with a bottle of wine will set you back around £60-70tel: 01328 710 209

The Three Horseshoes, Warham

The "Three Horseshoes" stands four-square on the crossroads at the centre of this village. It was formerly a shop property which owner Mr Ian Salmon has made into a very successful pub which serves superb food. Don't expect plush surroundings! It's bare boards and basic, but don't let that put you off. The awards from "Good Food" to Egon Ronay to Good Pub Guide won year-in year-out are countless, and the food is always top-notch home-cooking. It does get busy in-season (and out, sometimes!) There's ample parking space in the field diagonally across the cross-roads. A three-course meal for two with wine comes out at no more than £35-40. (I've lost count how many times my wife and I have been- and never been disappointed)

Beware: cards not accepted; cash only
stay here; B&b is available at the adjacent "Old Post Office" tel; 01328 710 547

The Red Lion, Stiffkey

Beside the main A149 is this village pub which does an excellent line in 'pub food Again I'll let its website speak
"The pub specialises in beers from East Anglia's top independent breweries, including Greene King Abbot Ale, Wolf Bitter, Woodforde's Wherry and 'pale, hoppy' Great Eastern. Food is also served and is stylish and filling. Local fish (from King's Lynn market) appears on the menu, Blakeney whitebait, soft herring roes on toast, crab salad and 'superbly fresh' grilled lemon sole. Other bar meals include salad of 'perfectly ripe' grilled goats' cheese, Thai spring rolls, chunky Norfolk game pie, and broccoli and Stilton quiche."Don't attempt to park at the front. A huge car-park has been (quite literally) carved out at the back.
more information: 01328 830 552

The Three Swallows, Cley-next-the-Sea

Good traditional pub food is on offer here in this pleasant inn overlooking the village green, and (mercifully) situated off the narrow, winding village street which is the main A149.
contact: 01263 740 526

The Cookies Crab Shop, Salthouse

Located by the side of, but just off the A149 road, you would almost miss this. Fresh seafood salads are served. You can enjoy these either in a wooden hut or out in the open. The prices are a bargain! The premises are unlicensed, but take your own alcohol (and glasses)
Fish salad with coffee or Norfolk fresh apple juice from £8 per head. This is a very populat
59
eating-place and it is strongly advised to book in advance
contact 01263 740 352

Byford's, Holt

Byford's has for long been a restaurant and delicatessen on the High Street of this bustling Norfolk town with its many byways and hidden treasures, when in the new dinner, bed and breakfast accommodation. Or else simply enjoy good food in the lively and convivial ambience of the restaurant. You can now stay in the modern deluxe b&b rooms
For more information tel. 01263 711400

Butler's Cafe, Bar, Restaurant, Holt.

Enjoy anything from a snack to a full meal at this newly-opened establishment. Produce is mainly seasonal and local.
More information: 01263-710790

Number 10, Sheringham

Under new management, this town-centre restaurant offers food to die for at prices that won't break the bank! Strongly recommended

NB You are advised to check on the status of this establishment

A designated area of Outstanding Natural Beauty

The North Norfolk coast is indeed an area of beauty, and it is also an area, where not only the beauty of God's creation can be enjoyed, it is an area of special interest on account of the abundance of wildlife. There is a whole range of nature reserves, some of which are listed below:

Blakeney Point (National Trust) It is home to a wide range of birds (some 270 species have been noted) and flowering plants, but best known for the seals, which breed here. They may be seen using one of the run from Morston an from Blakeney

Brancatser Marshes(National Trust) an area of salt marsh and Salthouse Marshes (Norfolk Naturalist Trust) is an extensive area of marshes protected by a high pebble defense-bank. It is a centre of observation with communications to 'twitchers' all over the country. Over 330 species of bird having been recorded here. Common attractions are avocet, bittern, common tern and marsh harriers and in winter also Brent geese, widgeon, teal and mallard.

Holkham Beach (Holkham Estate) is an extense of open sandy beach backed with dunes, on which pine trees have been planted to stabilise them. It is another possible site for bird watchers. Behind the pines is an area of salt marshes.

. Holme Bird Observatory (Norfolk Naturalist Trust) is an area of 90 acres behind the dunes between Thornham and Holme. Members may access by road from Holme. It is frequented by some rare migrant birds

. Morston Marsh (National Trust). An area of salt-marsh with many saltwater inlets.

.Sheringham Park (National Trust). This is an extensive area of woodland with many unusual tree species, such as Spanish Chestnut. Rhododendrons abound. There are many sign-marked walks.

. Titchwell Marsh Nature Reserve (RSPB) lies between the main A149 and extends out to the dunes and sand-flats. The RSPB have created a whole range of environments which are home to a wide range of bird species

THE NATIONAL TRUST

The National Trust manages quite large areas of the North Norfolk coast, especially those parts which comprise salt-marsh and has done much to preserve the environment, its wildlife habitat and also its amenities and facilities, which it is constantly extending and improving. Quite large areas have been improved and upgraded in time for the 2005 season The Trust has owns two properties on or close to this coast.

Sheringham Park

Sheringham Park comprises a large area of woodland garden, originally laid out in 1812 by Sir Humphrey Repton. There is a wide variety of trees growing here, including Spanish Chestnut, and flowering shrubs, such as azaleas and rhododendrons; these latter making a spectacular display in mid May-mid-June (depending on the individual season. The Park is criss-crossed by a number of way-marked walks, most extensive of which is the coast walk which takes the walker past the gazebo (from which magnificent views of a large stretch of coastal scenery are available) and past Sheringham House. This walk (which can omit the stretch down to Weybourne clifftop) is quite hilly and strenuous. Sheringham Park is crossed by the North Norfolk Railway. Sheringham Park lies just off the A148 road, about 2 miles southwest of Sheringham and 6 miles east of Holt. There is a car-park (£3 for non-Trust members), a visitor centre, which was upgraded during 2005. It is open to visitors from dawn to dusk seven days a week all year. The Visitor Centre is open from 1 March from 10am-5pm (4pm after 4 Nov), with a cafe open from 11am

Feldberg Hall

The Hall is one of Norfolk's finest 17th century mansions. If you visit the house you will see the 18th century furnishings, and see the single-artist Grand Tour paintings. Felbrigg also boasts a walled garden and parkland with waymarked walks. There is an NT shop, and tea room. There are also picnic tables in the car park (100 yards from the House). Felbrigg is 2 miles southwest of Cromer (signposts from the A140 from Norwich) and the A148 (from Sheringham) Entrance is (for non-Trust members) £7.00 (with concessions); £3.00 to gardens only. The Walks are open dawn-dusk, each day, all year, the Gardens Saturday-Wednesday from mid-March to the end of October Shop, Restaurant and Tea-Rooms are open 11.00am-4pm when the Gardens open, and 11am-4pm Thursday-Sunday up to Christmas. The House is open Saturday-Wednesday 1-5pm.

Coast

BRANCASTER. There is a large area, partly dunes backed by low-cliffs, partly slat-marsh, which is notable for its birdlife. The Trust cares for the marshes and mudflats, as well as the site of the Roman fort of Branodunum. There is a Millennium Centre. Scolt Island lies in the estuary from Brancaster Staithe, accessible by boat from Burnham Overy Staithe. There is limited parking at the Staithe and also (non NT) at the Brancaster Golf Club. (1 mile west) STIFFKEY is a stretch of salt-marsh and mudflats, with notable birdlife. Sea lavender grows on the marshes, and, in season, the local delicacy: samphire BLAKENEY NATIONAL NATURE RESERVE (which also incorporates MORSTON QUAY, 1 1/2 miles west). Almost all this reserve of 2711 acres is under NT ownership. There is a wide range of flora. Most notable, though, is Blakeney Point, a 3mile spit of shingle stretching west from Cley-next-the-Sea. This is home to breeding sea-birds as well as being populated for a while by passing migrants. The main visitor attraction are the seals. Boat trips are run for these from Morston Quay Parking is pay-and-display (£2.50) at Morston Quay (free for NT members). There is free landing on the Point which is also accessible by foot from Cley. (hard-going on the shingle)

WEST RUNTON, situated between Sheringham and Cromer, with very scenic conutryside stretching inland from the coast and including the highest point in Norfolk

(Information was correct for 2007- check with the Trust 'phone 0870-4584000) Note that the Trust is very dependent on volunteer workers; some facilities may now and again be closed)

NB Information on prices and opening times are for guidance only: check with the Trust

Travel to North Norfolk coast

North Norfolk's coast can only readily be accessed by road.

There are rail links, but they only touch the periphery of the area.   KING'S   LYNN situated some 20 miles south-west is at the terminus of a main-line route from London Liverpool Street.   HOLT is the terminus of the North Norfolk Railway: this connects via Sheringham with the main rail network from London. .   Travelling from the North and the Midlands is even more fraught.

Road access is better .   From the south via the A10 to King's Lynn.   From the Midlands via the A47 to King's Lynn From the North via the A17 to King's Lynn

All routes converge on King's Lynn (and thence diverge to Yarmouth/Lowestoft as well as North Norfolk). Roads around King's Lynn can be very congested, and beyond are slow. Allow good time for your journey if you are used to motorway travel!

The 'Coasthopper' buses offer a useful service along the coast- with a diversion inland to Burnham Market

All routes to North Norfolk converge on Kings Lynn and the 'Hardwick Interchange' , from where proceed north along the A149 for 3.6miles to the roundabout at the A148/A149 junction, from where-

To Brancaster:

Take the second exit on the A149 and continue for 4.4miles to roundabout – take first exit on to the

A149 (Dersingham Bypass) and continue 4.0miles to roundabout – take first exit to continue on A149 for 3.3 miles to roundabout – take 2nd (main) exit on the A149 and continue on the A149 past Hunstanton and in 2.1 miles come to Old Hunstanton. - keep on the A149 for 3.1 miles to Thornham – keep to the A149 for 1.4 miles to Titchwell – keep on the A149 and in 1.4 miles reach Brancaster.

To Wells-next-the-Sea:

Take the third exit on to the A148 and continue for 3.7 miles to Hillington – Keep ahead on the A148 for 6.9 miles to West Rudham – keep ahead on the A148 though the 30mph limit zone for 1.1 miles to West Rudham – keep ahead on the A148 for 5.0 miles to roundabout – take first exit along the A148 for 0.5 miles then left- join the B1105 for 10.4 miles to reach Wells-next-the-Sea.

For Sheringham:

take the route as for Wells, but do not turn off the A148; continue ahead and the A148 will lead you past Holt. After Holt continue along the A148 for 3.0 miles to Bodham – continue along the A148 for 1.6 miles- exit left on to the B1157 which leads in ca 3 miles into Sheringham.

Tourist Information Centres on or near the North Norfolk Coast

These are to be found at:
Burnham Market
Burnham Deepdale, PE31 8DD
Tel: (01485) 210256
Email: info@deepdalefarm.co.uk

Cromer
Prince of Wales Road
Tel (01263)

Fakenham
Red Lion House, Market Place
Tel: (01328) 851981
Email:info@eetb.info

Holt
Pound House, Market Place
Tel: (0870) 2254822
Email:holt@eetb.info

Hunstanton
Town Hall, The Green
Tel: (0870) 2254824
Email:hunstanton@eetb.info

Mundesley
Station Road
Tel: (0870) 2254834
Email:mundesley@eetb.info

Sheringham
Station Approach
Tel: (0870) 2254838
Email:sheringham@eetb.info

Walsingham
Shirehall Museum, Common Place
Tel: (01328) 820510

Wells-next-the-Sea
Staithe Street
Tel: (0870) 2254846
Email:wellsnextthesea@eetb.info

27140428R00045

Printed in Great Britain
by Amazon